09/24
STRAND PRICE
$ 5.00

Photography of the Fifties

Photography of the Fifties

An American Perspective

By Helen Gee

Funded by grants from

Ford Motor Company
National Endowment for the Arts

Center for Creative Photography
The University of Arizona/Tucson

Copyright notice for photographers' works:

Ansel Adams Copyright © Ansel Adams Publishing Rights Trust, 1980.
Richard Avedon: *Charlie Chaplin, New York City,* Copyright © 1959,
  Richard Avedon; *Isak Dinesen, Copenhagen,* Copyright © 1959, Richard
  Avedon; *Dwight D. Eisenhower, Palm Springs,* Copyright © 1964,
  Richard Avedon; *Dovima with Elephants, Cirque d'Hiver, Paris,*
  Copyright © 1955, Richard Avedon.
Wynn Bullock Copyright © Wynn Bullock and Edna Bullock Trust, 1980.
Harry Callahan Copyright © Harry Callahan, 1980.
Cornell Capa Copyright © Cornell Capa, 1980.
Imogen Cunningham Copyright © The Imogen Cunningham Trust, 1970.
Roy DeCarava Copyright © Roy DeCarava, 1980.
David Douglas Duncan Copyright © David Douglas Duncan, 1980.
Elliott Erwitt Copyright © Elliott Erwitt, 1980.
Andreas Feininger: *The Photojournalist,* LIFE Magazine, ©, 1955, Time Inc.;
  Coney Island on the Fourth of July, 1949, LIFE Magazine, ©, 1949, Time
  Inc.; *Pan Am Building,* Copyright © 1980, Andreas Feininger.
Robert Frank Copyright © Robert Frank, 1980.
William Garnett Copyright © William Garnett, 1954.
Ernst Haas Copyright © Ernst Haas, 1980.
Philippe Halsman Copyright © Philippe Halsman, 1980.
Lotte Jacobi Copyright © Lotte Jacobi, 1980.
André Kertész Copyright © André Kertész, 1980.
William Klein Copyright © William Klein, 1980.
Clarence John Laughlin Copyright © Clarence John Laughlin, 1973.
Leon Levinstein Copyright © Leon Levinstein, 1980.
Lisette Model Copyright © The Estate of Lisette Model, 1980.
Arnold Newman Copyright © Arnold Newman, 1980.

Irving Penn: *Black and White Vogue Cover:* Courtesy *Vogue,* Copyright ©
  The Condé Nast Publications Inc., 1950, 1978. *Harlequin Dress:*
  Courtesy *Vogue,* Copyright © The Condé Nast Publications Inc., 1950,
  1978. *Plumber, New York:* Courtesy *Vogue,* Copyright © The Condé Nast
  Publications Inc., 1951, 1979. *Woman with Roses:* Courtesy *Vogue,*
  Copyright © Les Editions Condé Nast, S.A., 1950, 1978.
Eliot Porter Copyright © Eliot Porter, 1980.
Aaron Siskind Copyright © Aaron Siskind, 1980.
Henry Holmes Smith Copyright © Henry Holmes Smith, 1980.
W. Eugene Smith Copyright © The Estate of W. Eugene Smith, 1980.
Frederick Sommer Copyright © Frederick Sommer, 1980.
Paul Strand: *Tailor's Apprentice, Luzzara, Italy, 1953,* Copyright © 1955,
  1971 The Paul Strand Foundation, as published in *Paul Strand: A
  Retrospective Monograph, The Years 1915–1968,* Aperture, Millerton,
  1971. *Women, Stes.-Maries-de-la-Mer, B.-du-Rhone, Provence, France,
  1950,* Copyright © 1976 The Paul Strand Foundation, as published in
  Paul Strand: Sixty Years of Photographs, Aperture, Millerton, 1976. *Hat
  Factory, Luzzara, Italy, 1953,* Copyright © 1955, 1971 The Paul Strand
  Foundation, as published in *Paul Strand: A Retrospective Monograph,
  The Years 1915–1968,* Aperture, Millerton, 1971. *Tir A'Mhurain, South
  Uist, Hebrides, 1954,* Copyright © 1962, 1971, 1976, 1982 The Paul
  Strand Foundation, as published in *Paul Strand: Portfolio IV,* Aperture,
  Millerton, 1982. *Cattle Sale, Loch Ollay, South Uist, Hebrides, 1954,*
  Copyright © 1962, 1971 The Paul Strand Foundation, as published
  in *Paul Strand: A Retrospective Monograph, The Years 1915–1968,*
  Aperture, Millerton, 1971.
Dan Weiner Copyright © Sandra Weiner, 1980.
Brett Weston Copyright © Brett Weston, 1980.
Minor White Copyright © Trustees of Princeton University, 1980.

Distributed by the University of Arizona Press
250 E. Valencia Road, Tucson, Arizona 85706

Foreword

As a general cultural phenomenon, the fifties have received due notice and investigation; however, photography has not received the same close scrutiny. Among Helen Gee's interests in curating the exhibition, *Photography of the Fifties*, and writing the accompanying essay, was her desire to bring forward for critical assessment a period in the history of photography for which she holds special curatorial qualifications.

During most of this period, Helen Gee provided the photography world with a sophisticated communal forum for the exposition of creative work. In May of 1954, she opened Limelight Gallery, a professional commercial exhibition space, in New York City (then the epicenter of the art world) at a time when institutional recognition and support of photography was still in its infancy. The gallery was supported by an adjoining coffeehouse, the combination of which provided a unique environment for photographers to gather together in an atmosphere of aesthetic interchange. Even by today's standards, the white walls, careful lighting, and individually curated shows were of the highest quality.

The general feeling of Limelight has been aptly described by Peter Bunnell (Carleton Gallery catalog, *Helen Gee and the Limelight*, February 12–March 8, 1977) as `` ... a meeting place and a socializing force for all photographers regardless of orientation ... however, Limelight was not the sort of place where a Jack Kerouac would have gone unless, of course, he had been taken there by one of his photographer friends, Walker Evans or Robert Frank. Limelight was a place of enthusiasm and friendship, not at all part of lonely Beat America.''

While Limelight provided Helen Gee with a unique perspective on the period, that of an active participant, her current essay and exhibition are about issues and forces in and upon photography of which the gallery was only a part. Her essay provides a retrospective overview of the period which includes more than just an academic report of the history and aesthetics of the photographers involved. It is a humanistic view which considers the works of the artists and the socio-political forces which affected their lives as inseparable. Her recall of the period is not nostalgic but analytical and inspired by insights privileged only to those who have endured the difficulties of having a vision before its time.

The Center for Creative Photography is deeply grateful to Ford Motor Company for providing the major funding for the *Photography of the Fifties* project. We also wish to acknowledge additional funding for the project provided by The

President's Club of the University of Arizona and the National Endowment for the Arts. In addition, we wish to thank the American International Sculptors Symposium for its help in the initial fund-raising efforts to sponsor the project.

We are indebted to the individual collectors, galleries, and institutions who generously placed works on loan for the exhibition, assuring a project of the highest quality. It should also be noted that the International Center of Photography in New York City, The Minneapolis Institute of Arts, The Art Galleries of California State University at Long Beach, and the Delaware Art Museum, through their participation, made a national tour possible.

Finally, we wish to express deep gratitude to the photographers whose generosity and interest in the project encouraged our efforts.

JAMES L. ENYEART
Director
Center for Creative
Photography

Photography of the Fifties By Helen Gee

Nostalgia for the past—even a past as recent as the 1950s—tends to obscure rather than illuminate the character and significance of a period. At a time in our history when looking back seems infinitely more comforting than looking ahead, nostalgia casts its romantic haze, softens the outlines and blurs the edges of hard historical fact. Television and a recent rash of musicals and films have contributed largely to the myopic view of the "fabulous fifties" as a time of calm and innocence, a period of social stability before the upheaval of the 1960s. It was the hula hoop, rock and roll, Marilyn Monroe, suburbia, TV dinners, family "togetherness," and eight years of Eisenhower. Americans played together and prayed together and, after the trauma of the Great Depression and two world wars, the American dream was realized at last.

Seldom are we reminded that the 1950s began not in a spirit of optimism but with a feeling of unease and apprehension. The end of the Second World War, contrary to expectations, had not banished the specter of a third yet more terrifying conflict. Peace, it appeared, was elusive. The "one world" we had envisioned was fragmented. Despite the United Nations, we remained locked in a non-combative struggle with Russia and suffered the mounting tensions of the Cold War. In 1949 Russia had already exploded its first atomic bomb and with that shock came the realization that atomic power could now be used against us. The arms race intensified, and as practice blasts were staged, fallout became an issue, despite the promise of a new "clean" bomb. Though Americans looked forward to potential benefits of atomic energy and to a time when each American home might be equipped with its own little nuclear generator,[1] it was hard to ignore Albert Einstein's warning of global destruction. Americans began to wonder whether there might be a future left to enjoy.

"Waging peace" became a national priority and, in 1950, when American troops were sent to Korea, a quick end was promised to what had first been reported as local skirmishes. Once again the face of General Douglas MacArthur in dramatic half-profile appeared in the press and, as the weeks and months dragged on, so did reports of heavy casualties. *Life* magazine, a prime conveyer of news and information, sent correspondents to the front to cover the story. In a photo essay published on Christmas Day, 1950, photographer David Douglas Duncan brought the horror of the undeclared war back to the coffee tables of America. Photographs of G.I.s fighting in the wasted terrain of Korea, not for villages but for hillocks—to be lost one day, regained the next, and lost again—shook the nation's confidence.

Meanwhile back home Senator Joseph P. McCarthy announced a "danger much greater than any threat from Communist Russia" was that of communists right here at home, lurking in our schools, factories, offices, even in churches and government.[2] No institution, organization or individual was beyond suspicion as McCarthy, Chairman of the House Un-American Activities Committee (HUAC), began investigations that were to ruin lives, wreck careers, endanger the democratic process, and cast a pall over the entire decade. Although anti-radicalism had been a recurring phenomenon in this country, seldom had it taken so virulent a form or had such devastating effects. Norman Mailer called the McCarthy period "one of the worst decades in the history of man."[3] If not one of the worst, it was one of the most shameful. If Western civilization was to survive, proclaimed McCarthy, the educational system had to be "scrubbed and flushed and swept clean.... "[4] Academic life suffered as teachers, guilty merely by association with suspected "fellow travelers," were fired. Libraries were searched for "subversive" material, and books such as Thoreau's *Walden* were seized and in some instances burned. Public hysteria surrounded the execution of accused spies Ethel and Julius Rosenberg.

The power of photographic imagery—its ability to reveal, conceal, explain, distort, to persuade and manipulate—had by mid-century rivaled the power of the pen. It was inevitable that photography came under the scrutiny of the House Un-American Activities Committee and that a likely target was New York's active and influential Photo League. Vulnerable because of its dedication to documentary photography, the Photo League was added to the Attorney General's list of subversive organizations as early as 1947. Although it managed to survive until 1951, blacklisting had substantially reduced its membership. The end of the Photo League represented the loss of "more than a camera club, more than a school." For many photographers, it was the loss of a "spiritual center."[5]

That the majority of photographers who were associated with the Photo League, either as members or as guest participants, were obviously not radicals is beside the point. That some undoubtedly were is also irrelevant. What is crucial, besides the threat that McCarthyism presented to artistic and intellectual freedom, was the effect these years of repression had on the visual arts and, in particular, on photographic imagery during the decade of the 1950s.

Robert Frank was one of the few photographers active at the time to describe his reaction to the period. Speaking of his travels through America on a Guggenheim Fellowship in 1955—the trip that resulted in his book, *The Americans*—Frank said, "Seeing those faces, those people, the kind of hidden violence—the country at that time —the McCarthy period—I felt it very strongly."[6]

Years earlier, Sid Grossman, the director of the Photo League's school, and an acknowledged radical, spoke about the personally painful years following the dissolution of the League and his subsequent harassment by the FBI. Remaining virtually in hiding, afraid of "the knock on the door," he complained of no longer feeling free to work on the streets.[7] He escaped as often as he could, seeking the solitude of Cape Cod. His work between 1948 and the time of his death in 1955 (at the age of forty-two) shows a clean break, a complete change in subject matter. From the lively images of rambunctious teenagers on Coney Island beaches he moved to contemplative scenes of sea and sand in Provincetown, a change which appears to be more psychological than geographic. While an extreme example of a shift from a documentary approach to a reflective, interior response to the world, it is symbolic of a change in sensibility that affected American artists, either consciously or unconsciously, during the decade of the fifties.

Attacks, such as those leveled by representative George A. Dondero on "Hobohemian chiselers,"[8] increased anti-intellectualism and supported the commonly-held view of artists as rebels. That artists could also be dangerous was suggested by a number of murals, presumably glorifying the proletariat, that had been painted in public buildings when, during the Depression, artists were employed by the WPA. Photographers, working for the Farm Security Administration, had also expressed their deep concern with social issues and had been bitterly attacked.[9]

Painting, however, by the 1950s had already taken another direction—one that, while it may have seemed puzzling, was, at least, less threatening. The Social Realism of the 1930s was now being superseded by the vanguard movement of Abstract Expressionism. Jackson Pollack, who had started painting as a Social Realist, was stunning the art world with his "spilled ink, spattered paint, and dripped pigment."[10] The bold new imagery of Willem de Kooning, Mark Rothko, and other painters of the New York School, while considered aesthetically revolutionary, was utterly devoid of social content as well as recognizable imagery.

In the discourse of the Abstract Expressionists, "action" no longer pertained to political action, but was the word used to describe the artist's relationship to the canvas. According to Robert Motherwell, the artists of the New York School were "apolitical, like cats."[11]

Photographers, on the other hand, were tied to the "real" world. Although some had turned to abstraction (most notably, Aaron Siskind, who was most closely associated with the New York School), many others felt that the nature of their imagery made them politically vulnerable. The dissolution of the Photo League had had a demoralizing effect. The trial of the Hollywood Ten, which had sent leading film directors and writers into professional limbo and jail, was a disturbing example of what might lie ahead for those producing slightly suspect imagery.[12] The impact on still photographers was more sharply felt in the East. West Coast photographers, who were nature-oriented and involved predominantly in formalism, were less deeply affected. The nude, the desert, and the Big Sur were hardly controversial.

For documentary photographers, it was a disaster. Lisette Model, who, as a European emigrée was acutely sensitive to the political climate, expressed their predicament. When recently asked about the fifties, she said, "It was terrible. You didn't know *what* to photograph."[13] The climate of McCarthyism undoubtedly affected the diminished output of many photographers and, for some, influenced a change of direction. Helen Levitt produced a film during the period, but this alone can hardly explain a nearly ten year lapse in still photography. Berenice Abbott turned to photo illustration of scientific principles. Marion Palfi moved from the plight of poor blacks to less politically charged problems of the aged. Dorothea Lange focused on the private world of home and family. As women, they may have felt a sense of double jeopardy at a time of political backlash. Walker Evans, secure on the staff of *Fortune* magazine, continued to work "in the manner of" Walker Evans, but lacked his earlier power. Paul Strand continued in full power but, like Charles Chaplin (who was persecuted for his political views) he chose to live abroad.

Opting for less controversial subject matter, rejecting grim social realities for more agreeable material, many photographers developed a more "humanistic" imagery. This changing imagery also reflected a change in the country's mood. Tired of tensions and problems, Americans turned to the benefits of a rising standard of living and concentrated on the comforts of the good life.

By mid-decade, the nation had recovered its equilibrium, and a new spirit of optimism prevailed. The Korean War was over. The Cold War continued, but showed little signs of heating. McCarthyism was on the decline. After five dishonorable years, the Senator had finally been censured by the Congress and removed from the House Un-American Activities Committee. Eisenhower's benign presidency assured the nation that all was well. For the first time since the war, the mood of the people caught up with the official optimism emanating from the White House.

In the photography world, this optimism was epitomized by Edward Steichen's *The Family of Man* which opened at The Museum of Modern Art in January 1955. The exhibition was conceived by Steichen as a testament to his belief in "the essential goodness of man" and, in keeping with the times, emphasized "human consciousness rather than social consciousness."[14] It was also meant as an anti-war statement and a protest against the use of the hydrogen bomb. After an exhibition of Korean war photographs at the museum had failed to arouse sufficient interest, Steichen decided on a large optimistic exhibition that would more likely get the message across.[15]

Unlike smaller shows he had displayed in the lower basement level of the museum, *The Family of Man*, which included 503 photographs taken by 273 photographers from 68 countries, filled the entire second floor. The exhibition was designed to lead the viewer past a maze of photographic blow-ups ranging in size up to ten feet and illustrating man's journey through life. Man (and woman), it appeared, were the same all over; natives of Somaliland played and prayed just like folks back home. Accompanying various photographic groupings were quotations from great literature and bibles of the world. Repeated throughout the installation was the photograph of a cheerful Peruvian piper sounding, ostensibly, the happy note that echoed throughout the exhibition.

The New York audience was enthralled, and the press jubilant. For the first time, photography overshadowed painting in the cultural limelight. Typical of the acclaim was a review in the *New York Herald Tribune* (January 30, 1955) that included this encouraging line: "It can truly be said that with this show, photography has come of age as a medium of expression and as an art form."

Jacob Deschin, the camera editor of the *New York Times*, and a persistent advocate of creative photography, showed somewhat less enthusiasm, describing the exhibit as "an editorial achievement rather than an exhibition of photography in the usual sense." (January 30, 1955.)

In an article titled "The Camera Versus the Artist" (February 6, 1955), Aline B. Saarinen, art critic of the *New York Times*, raised the question "has photography replaced painting as the great visual art of our time?" She concluded, "The answer is apparent. Painting is in our time, as it always has been in the hands of the giants, a great and strong means of expression. But photography is the marvelous, anonymous folk-art of our time."

Minor White, editor of the three year old quarterly magazine, *Aperture*, devoted an issue (Vol. 3, No. 2) to reviews and critical essays on *The Family of Man*. Among them was Barbara Morgan's rapturous description of the installation design. "The Birth bower is an open-sided circle suggesting emerging from the womb, the Death theme uses an open-ended tunnel, the rooms that lead to the H-Bomb are three sided cells, Religion and awakening Love are carried on running walls and a corridor, in keeping with the universals that keep life and hope continuing. In the Fun room pictures of eating, dancing and music are hung high. 'High spirits' literally 'raise the roof.'"[16]

Dorothy Norman, who selected the quotations for *The Family of Man*, defended her participation. She wrote, "The one thing that cannot be held against the Steichen exhibition is that it is not in the 'purist' tradition of Stieglitz. It does not pretend to be. It must be judged according to its own merits; for its own lacunae. It cannot be judged for what it is not."[17]

The single exception to the articles in *Aperture* basically praising *The Family of Man* was one by George and Cora Wright titled *One Fami-*

5

ly's Opinion.[18] Written in the form of a dialogue, each voiced the relatively silent dissatisfaction of a large part of the photographic community.

"I doubt that photographers would question the basic thinking behind the show," George Wright said, "if it had been designed for the lobby of the U.N. building." But, he asks, "Is it the function of a museum to hang a show which documents a particular social theme no matter how valid the theme is? Even if 'men are all men,' shouldn't a museum use its space to educate the public about photography as it does about the other arts?"

He then questioned the legitimacy of using single images, drawn either from a complete photo essay or from a photographer's whole body of work, to help illustrate a theme, with its consequent blurring of individual perception. "Any really great photographer, like a great painter, creates his own visual universe ... You can distinguish a Gene Smith from a Cartier-Bresson without a signature. You can instantly recognize an Adams, a Weston, a Laughlin print, or that of any mature worker whose previous work you've seen. They are all pointing lenses at the same universe but each selects the area or aspect which is most real to him. When we see a group of pictures made by these men, we enter his subjective world to look at reality through his eyes. But mixed up with others in a show, he surrenders his individuality...."

Cora Wright, in her part of the dialogue, admitted to having been overwhelmed by the exhibition, yet also having experienced mixed feelings. She, too, decried the subordination of individual statements to a dominating theme. "The Museum," she said, "doesn't use paintings in the same way—select 400 canvases to show a single theme. Why should photography be treated differently? Or is this a hangover from the old, ingrained idea that only the painter is truly creative while the photograph-maker, camera in hand, is just a selector who records?"

Both contended that, despite its failings, the show was impressive and, according to George Wright, "It could stand for a hundred things I don't believe in and I'd still be happy that it was put together." When Cora Wright replied that "the show's like a magazine essay. It's a contemporary use of photography," she touched on a crucial point—the extent to which editorial and journalistic concepts dominated photography in the 1950s.

It was Steichen who decided on the scale of the photographs, communicating his print specifications to a commercial lab that printed several editions that were to be exhibited throughout the world. The appropriation by a museum of decisions ordinarily left to the photographer demonstrated the general acceptance of the editor's role as applied, not only to magazine photography but, in this case, to an exhibition of photography as well. For purists to whom the quality of the print was as important as the image, this undoubtedly involved personal conflict. One could wonder about the reaction of

Wynn Bullock, whose small gem-like photograph, "Let There Be Light," was blown up to mural size. The loss of control on the part of the artist (not to mention the standardization of print quality) may have, in this case, had compensations. Bullock's photograph was chosen by a ballot of 64,844 visitors to The Family of Man at the Corcoran Galleries in Washington, D.C., as the most popular image in the show.[19]

The phenomenal success of The Family of Man, the enthusiasm with which it was received in cities the world over including Paris, Berlin, Tokyo, even Moscow, accomplished more for photography than was first realized. Behind Steichen's altruistic message lay another message, and this had to do with photography itself. What The Family of Man appeared to indicate was that photography was a universal language: as an expressive medium, it could communicate to the broadest range of people, it could cut across all lines of country and class, it was catholic, and it was democratic.

Photography's wide appeal had not gone unnoticed at the State Department. In the politics of the Cold War, in the battles for the minds and hearts of men, American culture was a weapon. Exhibitions of Abstract Expressionist art—then politically safe—had been sent abroad under various auspices. Aimed primarily at influencing European intellectuals, they proved that America was no longer a cultural backwater and showed how artists living in the "free world" were free to express their individuality. Those held politically suspect were excluded.[20]

The scope of Steichen's traveling exhibit dwarfed all previous cultural exports. It circulated for many years, was shown in more than thirty countries, and was viewed by over nine million people. Seen in this light, it can be said that The Family of Man did as much for American diplomacy as it did for photography.

Steichen, literally, placed photography on the map. Yet, ironically, it was the very success of The Family of Man that has obscured Steichen's full achievement during his fifteen years at The Museum of Modern Art. Identified with this "sentimentalized, utopian familial opus,"[21] his many smaller and more sensitively-handled exhibitions have been all but ignored. While the notion persists that Steichen's orientation towards photography was limited to humanistic photoreportage, the exhibitions he arranged after he first became director of the Museum's department of photography in 1947 covered a wider range. Over the years, he showed photographers as disparate as Harry Callahan, Henri Cartier-Bresson, Homer Page, Bill Brandt, Ralph Steiner, Frederick Sommer, Walker Evans, Edward Weston, Man Ray, Manuel Alvarez Bravo, August Sander, William Garnett, Aaron Siskind, W. Eugene Smith, Eliot Porter, Arnold Newman, Brassai, Ansel Adams, Todd Webb, Paul Strand, and historic figures such as Stieglitz, Lewis Carroll and Julia Margaret Cameron. Part of an East Coast photographer's education was seeing Steichen's exhibitions at The Museum of Modern Art.

Steichen was also an ardent supporter of women at a time when relatively few were working. He believed that photography was a medium particularly suited for women's intuition. "Intuition is simply keen perception and evaluation. They (women) know how to value their perception, which is something a man is very poor at, as a rule."[22] Among the women whose work he showed were Helen Levitt, Imogen Cunningham, Dorothea Lange, Lisette Model, and Margaret Bourke-White.[23] Also, his accessibility to young photographers, the encouragement he offered them personally, through exhibitions or purchase of their work for the developing Museum collection, served a crucial function during these early years.

The Museum of Modern Art, in addition to the George Eastman House, was a beacon in an otherwise barren landscape. Among the few traditional art museums that held occasional exhibitions of photography were the Cincinnati Museum of Fine Art, the San Francisco Museum of Art, and the Art Institute of Chicago. Museum exposure was important to those photographers who had few commercial outlets for their work, yet continued to represent a powerful current in the mainstream of photography during the 1950s.

Throughout the decade, photojournalism dominated the stage. *Life* magazine and, to a lesser extent, *Look*, were as much a part of American life as baseball and apple pie. Although television was becoming a major media force, it had not yet cut into the sale of magazines and newspapers. For millions of families, the weekly appearance of *Life* was as important as the weekly ritual of going to the movies. At that time, when society was simpler and offered fewer choices and expectations, the mass-circulated picture magazines held an importance and influence unequaled by any publication today.

Life was a presence. *Life* was reality. Photographs lent credibility and the voyeuristic thrill of being right there on the scene—on battlefields, in courtrooms, in living rooms—wherever the probing eye of the camera might wander. Some thought it was even "better than being there."[24]

Life's original manifesto read: "To see life; to see the world; to eyewitness great events; to watch the faces of the poor and the gestures of the proud; to see strange things—machines, armies, multitudes, shadows in the jungle and on the moon; to see man's work—his paintings, towers and discoveries; to see things thousands of miles away, things hidden behind walls and within rooms, things dangerous to come by; the women that men love and many children; to see and take pleasure in seeing; to see and be amazed; to see and be instructed."[25] Much of the material published, however, failed to live up to such noble aims.

Photojournalists were seen as free-wheeling, adventurous spirits "who traveled to far places, who met royalty and presidents ... who risked their necks in wars and sometimes got killed ... who dawdled in Hollywood with the world's most glamorous women ... who could go any-where and do anything ... "[26] While this may have been true of some photographers, a more accurate picture might have been that of a hardworking photojournalist performing under enormous pressure, often in difficult circumstances, who, after risking his neck, might see his story killed, or perhaps mutilated, by the editors who had the final say.

The photo essay, developed by *Life* and one of its most important contributions to photojournalism, was as much the creation of the editor as the photographer. Its final shape was determined by as many as seven people—writers, researchers, designers, and even advertisement space salesmen. From the point of view of the editors, the turn-of-the-century Eastman Kodak dictum could well apply: You Press the Button, We do the Rest. The exposed film was sent to *Life's* photolab; the negative editor made an initial selection; contact prints were sent to the picture editor, and so on along the line until the picture story was finally shaped and created. Many photographers saw their work for the first time when they opened the magazine.[27]

Not all photographers agreed to being "reduced to a robot, more a shutter-pressing piece of machinery than a thinking, feeling, seeing human being."[28] While this may have been an exaggeration, it illustrated the general nature of their dissatisfaction. The most famous of the malcontents was W. Eugene Smith.

Smith's uncompromising attitudes, and his in-sistence that he be fully involved in *Life's* editorial decisions involving his work, added to his reputation as a legendary photojournalist. Stories of his struggles with editors circulated throughout the photography world during the many years he worked for the magazine up to his final resignation in 1954.

During that time, he had won the right to choose his own assignments, and selected only those subjects that moved him deeply. *Life* had already discovered that the subjects that moved Smith also moved its readers.[29] His emotional response to the people he photographed, whether an obscure country doctor in the Mid-West or the renowned Dr. Albert Schweitzer in Lambaréné, was communicated in some of the most powerful photo essays ever to appear in *Life*. "The most important thing in photography," he said, "is knowing what the subject is about."[30] To get to know on a deeper level, he would often live with a subject for months before taking a single photograph. To prepare himself for his essay, "Nurse Midwife" (*Life*, December 3, 1951), he first took a two-week course in midwife training. While working on the story, he became so involved with the work of the clinic that he himself delivered a baby.

On his return from assignment, Smith would disappear into the darkroom and emerge weeks later—generally in a state of collapse—only after he was satisfied with each individual print. He would then throw himself into battle with *Life* and fight for a voice in the layout.

Smith's attitude toward his work was summed up in a talk he gave in conjunction with an exhibition of his photographs at the Village Camera Club in New York in 1952. When asked by a member of the audience, "What kind of lens do you use, Mr. Smith?" he replied, after a long pause, "Sir, I use the same lens used by Van Gogh."[31]

The sense of drama surrounding Smith may have excited the photographic community, but it was a trial for *Life's* editors. Despite their respect for his work, they were impatient with the long drawn-out saga each Smith assignment involved; a few more artists like Smith, and there would have been no weekly magazine. Speed was of the essence. Photographers had to be prepared to go anywhere, anytime, at the shortest of notice. *Life* had branches all over the world and a staff of crack photojournalists, including Alfred Eisenstaedt, Eliot Elisofon, George Silk, Nina Leen, Dmitri Kessel, Gjon Mili, Gordon Parks, Cornell Capa, John Dominis, Lisa Larsen, Andreas Feininger, Yale Joel, and Howard Sochurek. It also drew on the work of free-lancers and photographers associated with Magnum, Black Star and other picture agencies.

A sense of surfeit with high drama had begun to develop. There was now a place for the quieter, more introspective essays depending more on mood than action. Leonard McCombe's essay, "The Private Life of Gwyned Filling" (*Life*, May 3, 1949), which captivated the hopes and despair of a young career woman in New York,

marked the beginnings of a trend toward more subjective photojournalism. Later that year, *Life* published Smith's compassionate essay, "Country Doctor" (September 20, 1948).

These essays reflected a basic change. The rigid story line that characterized so many of *Life's* photo essays in the past, gradually gave way to a looser structure and a greater emphasis on mood and feeling. Formerly, bureaucratic editors might have laid out a story, suggested a lead picture, a closing picture, and planned in detail the sequence in between.

Edward K. Thompson, who became managing editor of *Life* in 1949, together with Charles Tudor and Bernard Quint, encouraged the freer format. It was during this period that Smith did some of his finest work, and the interpretive photo essay reached its highest point of development.

Smith's "Spanish Village" (*Life*, April 9, 1951) was a timeless study of a timeless part of the world. However, on first seeing the thousands of exposures Smith had taken during the year he spent in Spain, the editors were dissatisfied. There were few photographs to indicate the existence of Franco's police state. Smith's images showed more concern with birth and death cycles and eternal truths than with politics. In this respect, Eugene Smith can be considered the quintessential photographer of the 1950s. His influence, which paralleled the equally powerful influence of Henri Cartier-Bresson, was to affect a whole generation of young American photographers.

From time to time, *Life* used other artist-photographers. Dorothea Lange and Ansel Adams collaborated on the photo essay, "Three Mormon Towns" (*Life*, September 5, 1954); most of the photographs reproduced in the magazine were Lange's. She was again commissioned and produced her sensitive and lyrical essay, "Irish Country People" (*Life*, March 21, 1955). (Yet her "Public Defender," a picture story reminiscent of the social consciousness of her early work done for the Farm Security Administration, was rejected.)[32] "The Era of Sentiment and Splendor," a group of architectural photographs by Clarence John Laughlin, was *Life's* farthest departure from the classical photo essay. Although it completely lacked a story line, it was held together by both its theme and the photographer's haunting vision.

Under Thompson's direction, the magazine began to improve visually. Layouts were simplified, and stories less cluttered. It became a far cry from the early days of *Life* when "physically abused photographs" were "rounded, ovalized, or scalloped into cooky shapes ... cocked at precarious angles" and "given a rhomboidal trim or cut into the weirdest shapes of esoteric geometry,"[33]

However, despite these developments, *Life* had begun to lose much of the raw vitality of its early years. When it first appeared in 1936, it was unique; its success instantaneous. By the fifties, *Life* still reigned supreme, but had to compete with many other popular magazines such as *Look, Collier's, Coronet, Time* and *The Saturday Evening Post.*

"The urge to (sic) knowledge and information," wrote Eric Hogkins in a book about *Time* magazine, "seems to have become, in twentieth century man, almost a biological urge like hunger."[34] With food and the basic necessities no longer a problem (at least, not for the majority), leisure became a serious pursuit. There was a magazine for every interest—sports, culture, home decorating, fashion, beauty.

Women's magazines were widely read. Despite the fifties' emphasis on "togetherness," families were smaller and the divorce rate had accelerated. Women, many of them feeling isolated in their suburban homes, looked to magazines for advice on how to raise children, how to stay married, how to be happy and above all, how to be beautiful. *The Ladies Home Journal, Good Housekeeping, McCall's*, together with countless smaller publications, provided the answers.

Harper's Bazaar and *Vogue* were the aristocrats of the fashion world. The plainest woman could enjoy what Irving Penn once described as "a marvellous world which can be entered and experienced vicariously for only the price of a magazine. In that world there is no room for less than perfection; there women do not wrinkle as they age, fruit does not decay, babies do not cry ..."[35]

Alexey Brodovitch, the highly influential art director of *Harper's Bazaar*, brought the quality of life, however rarified, to this unreal world. Frozen contours of an earlier period of high fashion photography were metamorphized into a new image of women—individualistic, energetic, and in motion. Hemlines and buttonholes were sacrificed to the mood and spirit of the photographic image. Richard Avedon's photograph of a model in a couturier coat leaping over a puddle (*Carmen, 1957*), which he dedicated to the photographer Martin Munkacsi (who was the first to break the mold), indicated this new direction. Symbolically, it may also have suggested a freer stance for women, years before its time.

Teacher, mentor, innovator, and difficult taskmaster—Brodovitch's influence spread throughout the magazine field far beyond the pages of *Harper's Bazaar*. The total design concept he developed for the magazine was widely emulated. The photographers he published—Avedon, Lisette Model, Robert Frank, Bill Brandt, Brassai, Cartier-Bresson, André Kertész—were themselves major influences on photography both during the fifties and afterwards. Those he taught in workshop classes brought the benefits of his ''revolutionary eye'' to other publications, and to the field of advertising as well.

McCann Erickson, Young and Rubicam, and other leading agencies that made up the billion dollar business of advertising were still involved primarily with the printed page. The big swing to television came later. Commercial photographers were inundated with work. New York, the capital of the advertising world, involved a network of studios specializing in food, fashion, and a myriad of products that promised the good life and a sense of glamour.

Consumerism, after the deprivation of the war years, flourished. Newly-built factories churned out an endless array of goods. ''Built-in obsolescence'' shortened the life of many products and promised greater sales. The Kleenex culture—disposable everything—began to replace an earlier emphasis on thrift. Advertising stimulated an appetite for the new. Hemlines went up, then down. Cars spouted longer and longer fins. Consumers faced a dizzying array of soap powders, packaged goods, and other products in the larger, brighter, and more abundantly stocked supermarkets. The concept of credit spending supplied the means to buy endless goods. Consumerism was an abiding passion of the 1950s.

Not all photographers, however, shared the benefits of such consumer-oriented prosperity. Although much strong creative work was within the context of the magazine and advertising fields, many photographers chose to remain outside the commercial work—whether by inclination, temperament, or the nature of their work. The situation for them was at times bleak. The sole reward for years of uncompromising devotion to a personal vision was often simply inner satisfaction, and the esteem of their fellow artists.

Harry Callahan, who had several photographs reproduced in the 1953 *ASMP Picture Annual*, cryptically referred to such a personal decision when he commented on the works selected and said, "None were done on assignment."

Such thinking was relatively in isolation. By contrast, in May 1955, *Popular Photography* listed the results of an international poll which the magazine had conducted to determine who were considered *The World's 10 Greatest Photographers*. Compiled from the votes of "243 eminent critics, teachers, editors, art directors, consultants, and working photographers," the list was dominated by people-and-events-oriented East Coast photographers including, among others, Richard Avedon, Alfred Eisenstaedt, Ernst Haas, Philippe Halsman, Yousuf Karsh, Henri Cartier-Bresson, Gjon Mili, Irving Penn, W. Eugene Smith, and a West Coast exception, Ansel Adams. It is interesting to speculate on how this list would be revised were the same poll taken today. Substitutions might include several photographers who are eminently successful in today's gallery-and-museum scene, including Callahan.

For many fine photographers in the fifties, survival was the real question—not merely financial survival, but psychic as well. Some taught in colleges and art schools, which provided a reasonable living and allowed time for their creative work. Callahan, who started teaching at The Institute of Design in Chicago in 1946, was appointed head of its Department of Photography in 1949. His friend, Aaron Siskind, joined the staff in 1951, where both remained throughout the decade. In addition, others led the decade of the 50s as teachers. Henry Holmes Smith also taught at the Institute in 1938 and is known to the field as a dedicated teacher; he introduced one of the first university courses in the history of photography at Indiana University where he taught for thirty years. Ansel Adams founded the photography program at the San Francisco Art Institute in 1947 and began the annual workshops in Yosemite, which continue today. Ralph Hattersley and Minor White taught at the Rochester Institute of Technology, and Walter Rosenblum at Brooklyn College in New York; Lisette Model held private classes in her studio until 1952 when she joined The New School for Social Research in New York, where Berenice Abbott and Joseph Breitenbach also taught; Alexey Brodovitch's course in magazine layout photography was held in photographers' studios; and after the Photo League disbanded, Sid Grossman continued to hold small but high-powered sessions in his studio.

In general, photographers who taught favored the less structured atmosphere of studios and art schools to that of universities. Academia had not yet embraced the arts. Even if it had, photographers, no less than painters, would probably have seen such an embrace as a stranglehold. Formal education and degrees held much less significance in the art world of the fifties.

Another aspect of photographic education emerged in Rochester in 1947 with the establishment of the George Eastman House (now the International Museum of Photography at George

Eastman House). Beaumont Newhall was appointed Curator in 1948 and later became its most important director; Minor White joined the staff as Associate Curator in 1953. Together they established a coherent program for the preservation and exhibition of photographic art. Individuals who later made significant contributions to the field, such as Peter Bunnell and Nathan Lyons, acquired their professional expertise in the milieu of a then fledgling institution.

Minor White, whose aesthetic and philosophical concepts were antithetical to the upbeat humanism exemplified by Steichen's *Family of Man*, was in the vanguard of a movement that had not only a profound effect on his own photography, but came to symbolize important changes in American cultural attitudes of the 1960s. Both in his work and in his personal life, White stood for the private, interior, mystical (often esoteric) elements that ran counter to much of Western society. However, there were signs of a burgeoning interest in the philosophical concepts of the Far East advocated by White and others. An early indication was the underground popularity of Eugene Herrigel's *Zen and the Art of Archery*, a book discovered by the Abstract Expressionist painters, and one most surely familiar to White.[36] The romantic and mystical tendencies which attracted White to Buddhism found expression in his meditative sequential photographs, such as, *The Sound of One Hand Clapping*, 1959.

In addition to his work as artist and teacher, Minor White's aesthetic theories were imprinted in the successive issues of the new magazine *Aperture* which he edited for 24 years. Founded in 1952 by Minor White, Ansel Adams, Beaumont and Nancy Newhall, Dorothea Lange, Barbara Morgan, Ernst Louie, Milton Ferris and Dody Warren, it was the only American periodical at that time devoted to the aesthetics of photography. Without advertising or technical shop talk, *Aperture* depended on charitable contributions and received minimal support. It is ironic that it was the understaffed and undercapitalized magazine *Aperture*, with its handful of subscribers, that became such a pre-eminent and influential force in American photography.

The Swiss magazines *Camera* and *Du*, with their emphasis on contemporary and historical photography, were also an influence, as were *Image*, the in-house publication initiated by Beaumont Newhall at George Eastman House, and *Infinity*, the journal of the American Society of Magazine Photographers. The large popular magazines, *Popular Photography, Modern Photography*, and the now defunct *U.S. Camera*, which dealt primarily with technical know-how, had also begun to place more emphasis on creative aspects of photography.

Seen in retrospect, however, it was the appearance of *Aperture*, however quiet, that marked the beginning of a new period. Together with the much heralded *The Family of Man* exhibition, *Aperture* laid the groundwork for wider acceptance of photography as an art form.

It is worth pondering whether, without this pioneering work of the fifties, photography would have arrived at the high position it enjoys today.

Another milestone was represented by the debut of a gallery system for photography. Until the fifties, there had been none, since survival of a photography gallery through sales was impossible. Previous dedicated efforts—the Alfred Stieglitz galleries and the Julien Levy Gallery —were committed primarily to painting.[37] Nevertheless, the important exhibitions of photography held in these highly respected galleries had a twofold effect: photography was given a showplace, and its still disputed aesthetic value was given credibility when shown in the context of painting.

Limelight, the first gallery devoted exclusively to the exhibition and sale of photographs, opened in New York in 1954 and provided critical exposure for photographers for seven years. During that time, it was joined by two others—A Photographer's Gallery and Image. Limelight's purpose, as the name implied, was to bring photography into the limelight, and not have it share the stage with other visual arts. To solve the problem of financial support, the Limelight gallery was financed by the proceeds from a coffeehouse. However, to give it its own integrity, the gallery was constructed in a separate area. It was designed to hang up to 100 photographs and was run as any gallery would be today, with exhibition announcements, press previews, and a regularly changing schedule of exhibitions.

From 1954 to 1961, Limelight presented 61 exhibitions, including the work of Berenice Abbott, Ansel Adams, Bill Brandt, Brassai, Manuel Alvarez Bravo, Harry Callahan, Paul Caponigro, Imogen Cunningham, Robert Doisneau, Elliott Erwitt, Robert Frank, Isiz, Lisette Model, Eliot Porter, Aaron Siskind, W. Eugene Smith, Paul Strand, Edward Weston, and Minor White, among others. The work of younger photographers was most often introduced in group shows. Historical exhibitions included Eugene Atget, Julia Margaret Cameron, and Alfred Stieglitz.[38]

An average of two photographs were sold from each exhibition. Prices ranged from $25 for an Ansel Adams (including ''Moonrise, Hernandez'') to $50 for a Eugene Smith, $75 for an Edward Weston, and the astronomical figure of $125 for a Paul Strand. While in today's market these prices seem pitifully low, they were already an improvement on the past. Julien Levy never had a client for a photograph, and sold only a few photographs to friends for ''almost nothing.''[39]

Limelight exhibitions received extensive press notice, but the most serious and complete coverage was given by Jacob Deschin, whose reviews of photography over a period of many years provided major support to the field. In an article in the New York Times titled ''Galleries Needed'' (August 1, 1954), Deschin wrote, ''As of today there is only one gallery with a truly responsible attitude toward the medium related to a continuing program for showing photographs. It is Helen

Gee's Limelight Photo Gallery ... which made its debut in May ... ''

A year later, another gallery appeared. Roy DeCarava opened A Photographer's Gallery, converting a sizeable area of his apartment into exhibition space. During its two year existence, from 1955 to 1957, DeCarava showed the work of mature photographers, such as Ruth Bernhard, Sid Grossman, Walter Rosenblum, and Van Deren Coke. In 1957, he showed the work of Harry Callahan, which Deschin reported in the *Times* was the first comprehensive display of Callahan's over-all achievement to be shown in New York. In another series of exhibitions ''designed to encourage young talent'' (*The New York Times*, July 8, 1956), DeCarava showed Eugene Meatyard, Scott Hyde, David Vestal, Ted Tessler, Jay Maisel, Art Kane, and others.

A third gallery, Image (a semi-cooperative venture) was opened in 1959 by Larry Siegel and continued for two-and-a-half years. During that time, he made a major contribution by presenting the work of some of the finest young photographers emerging in the fifties; among them, Garry Winogrand, Dave Heath, Charles Harbutt, and Duane Michaels.

Norbert Kleeber's Underground Gallery was to follow in the 1960s and last for ten years, while showing photographers such as George Tice, Ken Heyman, and Bruce Davidson. During this same period, in 1969, Lee Witkin opened what was finally to become the first photography gallery able to sustain itself financially, independent of all other means.

The publicity surrounding the subsequent emergence of other financially independent galleries has obliterated one important fact. Since 1954 (with the exception of one gap of three years), New York has not been without a gallery devoted solely to the exhibition and sale of fine photography.

That photography's first gallery was supported by a coffeehouse illustrates the importance of the role of cafe life in the social and cultural milieu of the fifties. The run-down Cedar Bar achieved historic significance as the bailiwick of the Abstract Expressionists, centering around painters like de Kooning, Pollack, and Rothko. The White Horse Tavern found instant fame in literary circles when Dylan Thomas made it his New York hangout. Limelight, widely known for its gallery, had also become the meeting place for the photography world.

Every night of the week saw its share of visiting luminaries, photojournalists on the way to or from assignment, studio photographers at the end of a busy day, magazine editors, writers, art directors, and many others involved in the vast network of photographic enterprise. But it was also a gathering place for nonprofessionals—members of the progressive Village Camera Club and The Camera Club of New York, students and many ex-students of Lisette Model (who could be seen at a table almost nightly), and others who were equally concerned, not with assignments, but aesthetics. Many of them reflected Minor White's attitude as stated by Ralph Hattersley, "Photography has become closest to being a religion than anything else most of us have ever had."[40] One of the best of these nonprofessionals was Leon Levinstein, a former student of Sid Grossman who, working in the documentary tradition, has produced a major body of work over the past thirty years.

The sense of isolation that had set in with the closing of the Photo League disappeared in the congenial atmosphere of Limelight. Soon after it opened, coffeehouses became popular and what had long been a European tradition developed into an American phenomenon. Many of these coffeehouses became showplaces for guitarists, folk singers, jazz musicians, and poets.

Both in New York and San Francisco, poetry readings were a lively part of the coffeehouse scene. Allen Ginsberg, a guru of the new Bohemia, began to attract attention with his poetry. Yet, if it were not for the San Francisco police, Ginsberg might have remained just another local poet, and *Howl* just another long poem read to young audiences in the coffeehouses of the Bay area. But a raid on Lawrence Ferlinghetti's City Lights Bookstore brought the Beat poets into the public eye. Ginsberg's *Howl* was seized in 1956 with two other publications and declared obscene. A trial—and *Howl's* final vindication—attracted national publicity. As a consequence, Jack Kerouac's long-languishing book, *On the Road*, was published.[41]

At first, these "wild" and esoteric Beats, whose language violated everything that was thought to be good and true (and secure) in America, were taken as just another of the temporary California cults to hit the news media. But the Beats did not disperse like other fashions and trends. They were motivated by a deeper sense of mission. Their cause, which they considered essentially political, was an attack on the monolithic structure of bland, conservative, middle-class America.

The literary establishment, refusing to acknowledge an avant garde movement outside its domain, launched its own attacks. Beats, in their view, were "hostile to the mind, petulant toward tradition, and indifferent to order and coherence;" they howled when they had energy and when they didn't they sat around, beat and detached, in a funk.[42]

This stance was not entirely unattractive to the young, who had already adopted James Dean as a culture hero and were showing their own signs of rebellion. Juvenile delinquency was on the rise. Parents watched with alarm as Elvis Presley gyrated, and the hot beat of rock and roll replaced their own favorite "swing." The generation gap widened.

Blacks, whose ghetto rhythms had been preempted by the music industry, were uninterested in the Beats' use of "hip" jargon, and unimpressed by their professed identification with oppressed minorities. Jack Kerouac romanticized: "I wished (sic) I were a Negro, feeling that the best the white world offered was not enough ecstasy for me, not enough life, joy, kicks, darkness, music, not enough night ... "[43]

That insufficiency of feeling was the white man's burden was of no concern to blacks. The Beat Generation's glorification of violence got no hurrahs in the ghetto. Blacks were involved in a revolution of their own. A woman named Rosa Parks, refusing her seat to a white man, had triggered a bus boycott in Montgomery, Alabama. The Civil Rights Movement had begun.

It was 1955, and Robert Frank was on the road. His year of freedom, granted by a Guggenheim Fellowship, sent him on his now famous trip through America. The white line in his photograph, "New York, 1948"—a line dividing non-existent traffic on a deserted street —now stretched clear across the country. This image, picked up again in his photograph, "U.S. 285, New Mexico," taken on his transcontinental venture, became symbolic of a lonely and isolated America as filtered through Frank's urban sensibility.

Not since the westward movement of the 19th century had a photographer made such an in-depth attempt to photograph America independent of assignment, and completely on his own. Walker Evans, Dorothea Lange, Arthur Rothstein, Russell Lee, and other Farm Security Administration photographers had also made powerful statements while employed by that governmental agency, but were subject to the editing and guidance of Roy Stryker. In addition, the many photographers who had covered various aspects of the country since the 1930s did so while working for *Life*, or other picture magazines.

Frank's America was not *Life's* America; the official optimism that brightened *Life's* pages found no reflection in Frank's *The Americans*. The photographic world reacted strongly against his so-called bitter and jaundiced view. To nearly everyone's disappointment, the photographer who had often been called the poet of the camera, returned from his trip through the States with a photographic equivalent of T. S. Eliot's *The Wasteland*.

The images Frank found as he followed the white line—blanketed bodies of the dead on the roadside, crosses marking the scene of a crash, a lone baby with its jukebox nursemaid— symbolized an America, not of "togetherness," but of violence and spiritual desolation. This was not a popular view in the fifties, except among the Beats, with whom Frank could readily identify. Kerouac, in a rambling, eloquent introduction to *The Americans*, also saw " the humor, the sadness, the EVERYTHING-ness and Americanness of these pictures!"[43]

That these powerfully insightful photographs were made by a European living in America only a few years makes Frank's achievement even more remarkable. Seeing America with fresh eyes may have been an advantage, although Cartier-Bresson in photographing America never seemed to quite get under its skin. It is more likely that Frank's feelings of being an outsider, not merely as a European, but on a deeper level—a sense of personal estrangement—may have made him acutely sensitive to scenes of alienation and to images of disassociation. Frank's indecisive moments—the moments in between—did not result in that perfect configuration of chance elements that characterized the work of Cartier-Bresson. By comparison, Frank's photographs seemed almost artless.

The tentative feeling of so many of the images in *The Americans* conveyed something of the difficulty Frank faced while furtively photographing in roadhouse cafes or other places where the sight of a camera, especially in the hands of a foreigner, would hardly be welcome. In contrast to photographs which appear to have been casually made, others are reminiscent of his earlier work, and are carefully composed. These differences seem to suggest that Frank's approach was often a matter of circumstance rather than of design. Frank was the first to acknowledge his debt to Walker Evans, and would be the last to assume that it was his influence alone that caused what has since been recognized as revolutionary changes in the aesthetics of street photography.

At the time of Frank's trip, many photographers were already experimenting with blurs, graininess, and unconventional cropping. William Klein, who worked in New York in 1954 and 1955, was an important influence on many of these young photographers. His brash, hard-hitting images were published in a book he designed himself with the improbable title, *Life is Good and Good for You in New York William Klein Trance Witness Revels*. Like *The Americans*, the book was published in France where Klein lived as an American expatriate and, like Frank, he eventually abandoned still photography (in 1965) and turned to film.

The fact that Frank's *Americans* and Klein's *New York* were both published abroad was no coincidence. The chances of finding a publisher for photographs even less controversial than these were slim. *Aperture* eventually expanded its activities and established a standard of excellence for book design and reproduction, but not until the 1960s when it released *Frederick Sommer Photographs, 1939–1962* in 1963, and *Edward Weston: The Flame of Recognition* in 1965. Few photography books except manuals on technique appeared to find a market. The one exception was *The Family of Man*, a book that included all of the photographs that had appeared in the exhibition, and sold in the millions.

Meanwhile, the big picture magazines had begun to decline. In 1957, *Collier's* was the first to fail. Others that had once been a major outlet for photographers' work also succumbed— *Coronet* in 1961, *The American Weekly* in 1963, *This Week* in 1969, and *Look* in 1971. *Life*, which for a quarter of a century had been the most widely read and influential magazine in the country, folded in 1972. Staff photographers, naturally, lamented its loss. Others, recognizing that *Life* had lost both its vitality and its purpose, had long seen it as some large woolly mammoth doomed to extinction.

It was the end of an era. The excitement that *Life* once generated following its promise "to eyewitness great events ... to see strange things ... in the jungle ... and on the moon ... " palled in the face of television's more immediate and comprehensive coverage. A visit to far-off places via the second-hand route of the magazines was now done first-hand by jumping on a plane. A generation raised on television found photo essays incomplete and out-of-date.

The youth culture of the sixties had emerged. The restlessness of the fifties turned into the political activism of the 1960s. America was shaken out of its earlier passivity through the Vietnam anti-war protest, the birth of the New Left, the sexual revolution, increasing black militancy, growth of Women's Liberation and, in its negative aspects, the spread of the drug culture. Dylan's song, "The Times They Are A'Changin'," applied to the whole of American society, including photography. It, too, had begun to change.

The rise of television and the loss of the magazines had a profound effect on photographic imagery. With its role as a witness of the world usurped, photography turned inward. Young photographers looked attentively at the work of inner-oriented image-makers like Frederick Sommer, who, since he began to photograph in 1936, had remained outside the mainstream. Sommer's involvement with Surrealism, the found object, and his interest in the elements of accident and chance, appealed to a generation that rejected the blueprint approach

to existence and was consulting the *I Ching*. "Poetic and speculative photographs," Sommer said, "can result if one works carefully and accurately, yet letting chance relationships have full play."[44] This also appealed to photographers working in the tradition of photo reportage who began to see America as increasingly surreal.

Sommer's highly experimental work— making photographs, at one point, without a camera (as did Henry Holmes Smith)—was an anachronism in the fifties when manipulating an image was considered almost a cardinal sin. Even Eugene Smith, when in order to obtain certain effects, applied handwork to a print, did it rather surreptitiously and only talked openly about it once it became acceptable.

Although Minor White's work derived from the Stieglitz-Strand-Weston tradition of "straight" photography, his symbolist, metaphorical images were to have a profound effect on the new developing imagery. Aaron Siskind (who, like Sommer, homed in on the found object) and another formalist, Harry Callahan, enjoyed increasing recognition as photographers and teachers.

Although for many years and during the fifties these photographers worked outside the mainstream, they nevertheless represented powerful currents in the overall scene. Paul Strand and Ansel Adams stood for decades like monumental rocks in the landscape of American photography. Their influence has been incalculable. During this period, Eliot Porter, who also lived and worked outside New York, brought a rare sensibility to the use of color at a time when its aesthetic application still lagged far behind black and white photography.

While mainstream photographers were less consciously involved in making art, they were nevertheless acutely aware of and influenced by the work of these artist-photographers. Also during this increasingly art-conscious decade, many photographers involved with commercial work and reportage were motivated to bring strong elements of creativity into their work. This led to a cross-fertilization of ideas, techniques, and experimental approaches to the medium.

The period was further enriched by the interaction between American photographers and the more recently arrived Europeans such as the influence of Walker Evans on Robert Frank and that of Lisette Model on Diane Arbus. Many American photographers working in the field of reportage looked to the work of Henri Cartier-Bresson. His book, *The Decisive Moment*, published in 1952, influenced the fifties as much as Robert Frank's *The Americans* was to affect the sixties and seventies.

European ideas had a powerful effect during the fifties. Existentialism and the writings of Jean Paul Sartre, Albert Camus, Simone de Beauvoir, Martin Buber and Teilhard de Chardin were all part of intellectual fare. Earlier, in the 1940s, a number of painters had become involved with the idea of the unconscious through the psychoanalytical theories of Sigmund Freud and moved from Social Realism to Abstract Expressionism. This presaged a dominant trend in the 1950s—the shift from Marx to Freud. Photography moved in a similar but not parallel path, from the dominance of documentary (with its social involvement) to an emphasis on more subjective forms of expression. The transition was more subtle and the timing different.

The high interest in artist-photographers today is paralleled by the growth of a more sophisticated audience of museum and gallery goers, a transition started in the fifties. Certainly domination by magazines then often represented a hazard for the serious photographer. In today's sympathetic environment different hazards exist—in working for gallery exposure, being shaped by overly scholastic attitudes, and following established trends.

Yet in all periods, art has represented risk, no less to itself than to the society it reveals.

ACKNOWLEDGEMENTS

In taking this look back at the fifties, I have had the pleasure and privilege of working with James L. Enyeart, Director of the Center for Creative Photography and the Center's staff. The fund of knowledge Mr. Enyeart brought to this project, combined with his directorial abilities, made this association extremely satisfying. I wish to extend special thanks to Sandy Schwartz, Registrar for the Center; Marguerite McGillivray, Administrative Assistant; Minnette Burges, Editorial Assistant; Sherrie Denton and Jan Stevenson, Curatorial Assistants; Linda Fry, Photographer; and Terence Pitts, Curator, for their dedicated and invaluable assistance.

I am also indebted to Sally Stein, Cora Wright Kennedy, Carol Brower, Dori Lewis and Janet Rozine for lending their own special expertise to the project. To those photographers, both known and unknown, who contributed to the important period of the 1950s, my respect and admiration.

H. G.

Notes

1. Douglas T. Miller and Marion Nowak, *The Fifties: The Way We Really Were* (Garden City, New York: Doubleday & Company, Inc., 1975), p. 48. RCA's David Sarnoff predicted the use of small home generators and atomically fueled automobiles before 1980.

2. Senator Joseph P. McCarthy, *McCarthyism, The Fight for America* (New York, New York: The Devin-Adair Company, Publishers, 1952), p. 101.

3. Miller and Nowak, *op. cit.,* p. 6, citing John Montgomery, *The Fifties* (London, 1965). Norman Mailer is quoted on the title page.

4. McCarthy, *op. cit.,* p. 101.

5. Dr. Fritz Neugass, "Photo-League, New York," *Camera* (September, 1950), p. 264.

6. Eugenia Parry Janis and Wendy MacNeil, *Photography Within the Humanities* (New Hampshire: Addison House, 1977), p. 54.

7. Author's conversation with Anne Tucker, 1979, quoting Sid Grossman. Other information based on author's conversations with Grossman, 1952.

8. Dore Ashton, *The New York School* (New York: The Viking Press, 1972), p. 64.

9. Jacquelyn Judge, "F.S.A. Attacked," *Photo Notes* (Fall, 1948), no pagination.

10. Robert Brustein, "The Cult of Unthink," *Horizon* (September, 1958), p. 38.

11. Max Kozloff, "An Interview with Robert Motherwell," *Artforum* (September, 1965), p. 37.

12. Miller and Nowak, *op. cit.,* p. 316. More than 500 actors, directors, writers, and producers were blacklisted in Hollywood, many unable to work again.

13. Author's conversation with Lisette Model, 1979.

14. Jerry Mason, editor, *The Family of Man* (New York: The Museum of Modern Art, 1955), p. 5.

15. Robert E. Hood, *12 at War* (New York: G. P. Putnam's Sons, 1967), p. 76. "In his third attempt to dramatize the stupidity of war, he produced an exhibition on the Korean War, which he considered had been more realistically interpreted than any previous war. Dominating the exhibition were the powerful photographs of David Douglas Duncan. 'People flocked in great numbers to see it,' Steichen recalled. 'They found some pictures revolting, some deeply moving, there were even some tears shed, but that is as far as it went. They left the exhibition and promptly forgot it.' He concluded his approach was wrong—too negative— what was needed was a positive approach ... This was the seed for perhaps the most awesome photographic exhibition ever attempted."

16. "The Controversial Family of Man," *Aperture* (1955), section by Barbara Morgan, pp. 24–27

17. *Ibid.,* section by Dorothy Norman, pp. 12–16

18. *Ibid.,* section by George and Cora Wright, pp. 19–23.

19. Conversation with Edna Bullock.

20. Eva Crockcroft, "Abstract Expressionism, Weapon of the Cold War," *Artforum* (June, 1974), pp. 39–41. The American Federation of Arts refused to withdraw the work of ten artists considered politically unacceptable from a major exhibition, *100 American Artists,* it was organizing for the U.S. Intelligence Agency. The USIA consequently cancelled the exhibition.

21. Alan Sekula, "The Instrumental Image: Steichen at War," *Artforum* (December, 1975), p. 35.

22. Milton Meltzer, *Dorothea Lange: A Photographer's Life* (New York: Farrar, Straus, Giroux, 1978), p. 337.

23. *Six Women Photographers: Margaret Bourke-White, Helen Levitt, Dorothea Lange, Tana Hoban, Hazel Frieda Larsen and Esther Bubley* was shown at the Museum of Modern Art in 1949. Others appeared in group shows and *The Family of Man.*

24. Wilson Hicks, *Words and Pictures* (New York: Harper & Brothers, 1952), p. 11.

25. Maitland A. Edey, *Great Photographic Essays from Life* (Boston: New York Graphic Society, 1978), p. 4.

26. *Ibid.,* p. 13.

27. *Ibid.,* see essay on history of *Life* magazine, pp. 1–21.

28. Margery Mann, "Review of Paul Hassel exhibition, San Francisco Museum," *Artforum* (June, 1960), p. 59.

29. Dora Jane Hamblin, *That Was The Life* (New York: W. W. Norton & Company, Inc., 1977) pp. 282–283. After publication of Smith's photo essay, "Nurse Midwife," readers donated enough money to build midwife Maude Callen's new clinic.

30. Author's conversation with W. Eugene Smith, mid-fifties.

31. Author present at lecture.

32. Meltzer, *op. cit.,* p. 279. Lange claimed "Public Defender" was rejected because it was not journalistic, that it represented all rather than a particular defender in a particular case.

33. Hicks, *op. cit.,* pp. 42–43.

34. *Ibid.,* quoting Eric Hodgins, *The Span of Time, A Primer History of Time Incorporated* (New York: Time, Inc., 1946), p. 45.

35. Alexander Liberman, editor, *The Art and Technique of Color Photography* (New York: Simon & Schuster, 1951), p. 2.

36. Author was introduced to the book by Eliot Porter in 1957.

37. Stieglitz' "291" and the Julien Levy Gallery stressed photography initially but after the first few seasons turned primarily to the exhibition of paintings.

38. *Helen Gee and the Limelight: A Pioneering Gallery of the Fifties,* exhibition catalogue, Carlton Gallery, New York, New York, (February 12–March 8, 1977). Includes chronology.

39. *The Julien Levy Collection,* exhibition catalogue, The Witkin Gallery, Inc., New York, New York, no pagination.

40. Minor White, *Octave of Prayer* (Millerton, New York, 1972), quoting Frank Hattersley, p. 91.

41. Miller and Nowak, *op. cit.,* pp. 383–384.

42. Brustein, *op. cit.,* quoting Jack Kerouac, p. 41.

43. Robert Frank, *The Americans* (New York: Grove Press, 1959), Introduction by Jack Kerouac, p. ii.

44. Gerald Nordland, *Frederick Sommer: An Exhibition of Photographs,* exhibition catalogue, Philadelphia College of Art (November 1–30, 1968), p. 13.

Photography of the Fifties

LISETTE MODEL

LISETTE MODEL   Sammy's Bar, New York, 1950.   48.1 x 39.4 cm.   Courtesy of The Sander Gallery, Washington, D.C.   27

28   LISETTE MODEL   *New York, ca. 1958.*   39.1 x 49.5 cm.   Courtesy of The Center for Creative Photography, Tucson.

LISETTE MODEL   New York, 1940.   48.9 x 38.9 cm.   Courtesy of The Center for Creative Photography, Tucson.   29

MINOR WHITE

MINOR WHITE   For Edward Weston, January 3, 1958.   18.9 x 24.4 cm.   Courtesy of Harry H. Lunn, Jr.   31

32 MINOR WHITE   Frost Wave, 1959, from the sequence *Sound of One Hand Clapping,* 1959.   34.1 x 24.5 cm.   Courtesy
of The Minor White Archive, Princeton University.

MINOR WHITE   Two Barns and Shadow, 1955, from *Rural Chapels, Sequence 10,* 1955.   23.6 x 30.4 cm.   Courtesy of The   33
Minor White Archive, Princeton University.

34 MINOR WHITE   Metal Ornament, 1957, from the sequence *Sound of One Hand Clapping,* 1959.   18.5 x 23.1 cm.
Courtesy of The Minor White Archive, Princeton University.

ANDRÉ KERTÉSZ

36   ANDRÉ KERTÉSZ   42nd Street and First Avenue, 1951.   17.9 x 24.8 cm.   Courtesy of the photographer.

ANDRÉ KERTÉSZ   MacDougal Alley, 1950.   20.9 x 16.9 cm.   Courtesy of the photographer.   37

38   ANDRÉ KERTÉSZ   10th Street, 1960.   24.7 x 19.8 cm.   Courtesy of the photographer.

ARNOLD NEWMAN

40   ARNOLD NEWMAN   Jackson Pollock, 1949.   26.5 x 20.9 cm.   Courtesy of Light Gallery, New York.

ARNOLD NEWMAN   Willem de Kooning, 1959.   27.0 x 31.5 cm.   Courtesy of Light Gallery, New York.   41

42   ARNOLD NEWMAN   Erhard Weyhe in his Bookshop and Gallery, 1952.   14.3 x 24.6 cm.   Courtesy of Light Gallery, New York.

ARNOLD NEWMAN   Brooks Atkinson, Morosco Theater, 1951.   33.5 x 26.8 cm.   Courtesy of Light Gallery, New York.   43

ANDREAS FEININGER

ANDREAS FEININGER   The Photojournalist, 1955.   34.4 x 26.5 cm.   Courtesy of the photographer.   45

46   ANDREAS FEININGER   Coney Island on the Fourth of July, 1949.   26.6 x 34.1 cm.   Courtesy of the photographer.

ANDREAS FEININGER   Pan Am Building, ca. 1960.   34.2 x 26.7 cm.   Courtesy of the photographer.   47

DAVID DOUGLAS DUNCAN

DAVID DOUGLAS DUNCAN   Korea, 1950.   33.5 x 49.2 cm.   Courtesy of The Museum of Modern Art, gift of the   49
photographer.

50 DAVID DOUGLAS DUNCAN   Marine, Korea, 1950.   45.7 x 50.1 cm.   Courtesy of The Museum of Modern Art, gift of the photographer.

DAVID DOUGLAS DUNCAN   Korea, 1950.   33.8 x 23.0 cm.   Courtesy of The Museum of Modern Art, gift of the   51
photographer.

ROY DE CARAVA

ROY DE CARAVA   Woman and Children at Intersection, Harlem, ca. 1950.   23.8 x 32.5 cm.   Courtesy of the Witkin Gallery,   53
New York.

54 ROY DE CARAVA Haynes, Jones, and Benjamin, ca. 1950. 22.9 x 32.7 cm. Courtesy of The Witkin Gallery, New York.

ROY DE CARAVA   Coltrane and Elvin, ca. 1950.   25.2 x 32.8 cm.   Courtesy of The Witkin Gallery, New York.   55

56 ROY DE CARAVA Two Women, Mannequin's Hand, ca. 1950. 24.5 x 32.7 cm. Courtesy of The Witkin Gallery, New York.

ERNST HAAS

58   ERNST HAAS   Moon Glow, New York City, 1959.   48.9 x 31.9 cm.   Courtesy of the photographer.

ERNST HAAS   Egyptian Boys, 1956.   33.4 x 49.4 cm.   Courtesy of the photographer.   59

HARRY CALLAHAN

HARRY CALLAHAN   Eleanor, Port Huron, 1954.   18.0 x 17.7 cm.   Courtesy of The Center for Creative Photography, Tucson.   61

62   HARRY CALLAHAN   Collages, ca. 1956.   19.4 x 24.4 cm.   Courtesy of Light Gallery, New York.

HARRY CALLAHAN   Randolph Street, Chicago, 1956.   20.5 x 31.0 cm.   Courtesy of Light Gallery, New York.   63

64   HARRY CALLAHAN   Chicago, 1950.   19.9 x 29.5 cm.   Courtesy of The Center for Creative Photography, Tucson.

HARRY CALLAHAN   Chicago, 1958.   19.3 x 29.8 cm.   Courtesy of Light Gallery, New York.   65

CLARENCE JOHN LAUGHLIN

CLARENCE JOHN LAUGHLIN   The Solidity of Shadows (No. 1), 1953.   27.2 x 34.8 cm.   Courtesy of The Robert Miller   67
Gallery, New York.

68   CLARENCE JOHN LAUGHLIN   In Magical Light (No. 1), 1953.   34.6 x 27.3 cm.   Courtesy of The Robert Miller Gallery, New York.

CLARENCE JOHN LAUGHLIN   A Vision of Dead Desire, 1954.   34.6 x 24.2 cm.   Courtesy of The Robert Miller Gallery,   69
New York.

W. EUGENE SMITH

W. EUGENE SMITH   Death of Gus-Gus, from the essay "Juanita," 1953.   26.0 x 33.2 cm.   Courtesy of The Estate of   71
W. Eugene Smith.

72 W. EUGENE SMITH Spanish Women, from the essay ''Spanish Village,'' 1951. 34.6 x 24.1 cm. Courtesy of The
Estate of W. Eugene Smith.

W. EUGENE SMITH   Schweitzer at the Lamp, from the essay "Man of Mercy," 1954.   26.8 x 41.0 cm.   Courtesy of the Estate   73
of W. Eugene Smith.

74   W. EUGENE SMITH   Devil Goggles, from the essay ''Pittsburgh,'' 1955.   22.2 x 31.6 cm.   Courtesy of The Estate of W. Eugene Smith.

W. EUGENE SMITH Waiting for Survivors, Andrea Doria, 1956.   16.0 x 25.3 cm.   Courtesy of The Estate of W. Eugene Smith.   75

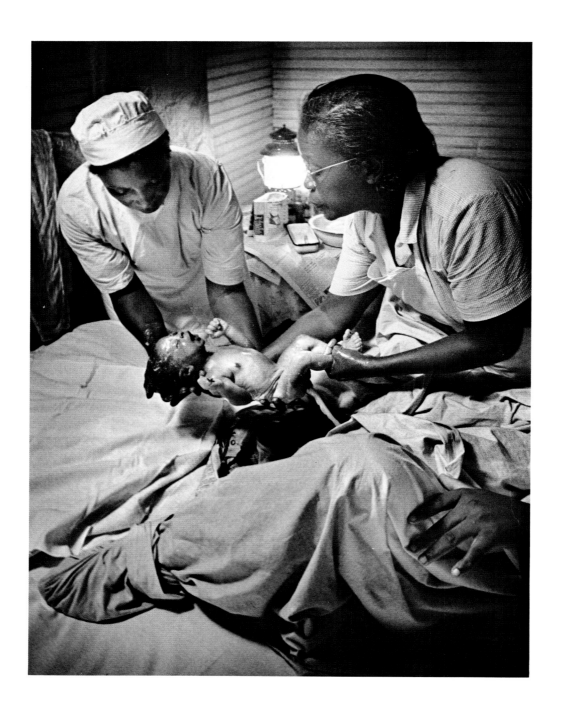

76 W. EUGENE SMITH Maude, Delivery, from the essay "Nurse Midwife," 1951. 33.8 x 25.5 cm. Courtesy of The Estate of W. Eugene Smith.

LOTTE JACOBI

78   LOTTE JACOBI   Dimensions No. 4, ca. 1950.   32.3 x 25.3 cm.   Courtesy of Light Gallery, New York.

LOTTE JACOBI   Butterflies, ca. 1950.   31.5 x 25.7 cm.   Courtesy of Light Gallery, New York.   79

RICHARD AVEDON

RICHARD AVEDON   Charlie Chaplin, New York City, 1952, from the *Minneapolis Portfolio,* 1970.   45.0 x 60.8 cm.   81
Courtesy of the photographer.

82 RICHARD AVEDON   Isak Dinesen, Copenhagen, 1958, from the *Minneapolis Portfolio,* 1970.   58.4 x 50.7 cm.
Courtesy of the photographer.

RICHARD AVEDON   Dwight D. Eisenhower, Palm Springs, 1964, from the *Minneapolis Portfolio,* 1970.   83
55.7 x 50.8 cm.   Courtesy of the photographer.

84 RICHARD AVEDON Dovima with Elephants, Cirque d'Hiver, Paris, 1955, from a limited edition, 1955. 58.3 x 46.9 cm.
Courtesy of the photographer.

BRETT WESTON

86 BRETT WESTON (Untitled), 1953. 19.3 x 24.4 cm. Courtesy of The Center for Creative Photography, Tucson.

BRETT WESTON   Black Window, 1950.   26.4 x 34.4 cm.   Courtesy of The Center for Creative Photography, Tucson.   87

WYNN BULLOCK

WYNN BULLOCK   Let There Be Light, 1954.   18.8 x 24.2 cm.   Courtesy of Edna Bullock.   89

90   WYNN BULLOCK   Navigation Without Numbers, 1957.   18.3 x 23.0 cm.   Courtesy of Edna Bullock.

WYNN BULLOCK   The Pilings, 1958.   19.0 x 23.5 cm.   Courtesy of Edna Bullock.   91

AARON SISKIND

AARON SISKIND   Chicago 42, 1952.   35.1 x 44.7 cm.   Courtesy of the photographer.   93

94   AARON SISKIND   Kentucky, 1949.   35.8 x 44.2 cm.   Courtesy of Light Gallery, New York.

AARON SISKIND   St. Louis 9, 1953.   26.4 x 33.5 cm.   Courtesy of Light Gallery, New York.   95

96   AARON SISKIND   Chicago 206, 1953.   34.0 x 41.5 cm.   Courtesy of The Center for Creative Photography, Tucson.

AARON SISKIND   Number 491, from the portfolio *Terrors and Pleasures of Levitation,* 1954.   25.0 x 24.2 cm.   Courtesy of   97
The Center for Creative Photography, Tucson.

ELLIOTT ERWITT

ELLIOTT ERWITT   Las Vegas, 1957.   20.2 x 30.4 cm.   Courtesy of the photographer.   99

100   ELLIOTT ERWITT   Hollywood, 1956.   40.5 x 27.1 cm.   Courtesy of the photographer.

ELLIOTT ERWITT   Oakland, 1955.   20.3 x 30.2 cm.   Courtesy of the photographer.   101

CORNELL CAPA

CORNELL CAPA   Adlai Stevenson Campaign, 1956.   23.5 x 34.1 cm.   Courtesy of the photographer.   103

104   CORNELL CAPA   Adlai Stevenson, Boston Airport, 1956.   35.7 x 44.3 cm.   Courtesy of the photographer.

CORNELL CAPA   Adlai Stevenson Campaign, 1956.   34.1 x 23.5 cm.   Courtesy of the photographer.   105

PHILIPPE HALSMAN

PHILIPPE HALSMAN   Marilyn Monroe with Dumbbells, 1952.   27.8 x 35.2 cm.   Courtesy of The Hastings Galleries,   107
New York.

108 PHILIPPE HALSMAN   Peep Show Bubble Bath, Philadelphia, 1950.   27.3 x 34.5 cm.   Courtesy of The Hastings Galleries, New York.

PHILIPPE HALSMAN   Consumer Products, ca. 1950.   32.8 x 27.1 cm.   Courtesy of The Hastings Galleries, New York.   109

LEON LEVINSTEIN

LEON LEVINSTEIN   Tatooed Man, 1958.   44.1 x 38.2 cm.   Courtesy of the photographer.   111

112   LEON LEVINSTEIN   Coney Island, 1959.   39.8 x 50.9 cm.   Courtesy of the photographer.

LEON LEVINSTEIN   Fifth Avenue, 1958.   42.6 x 35.1 cm.   Courtesy of the photographer.   113

PAUL STRAND

PAUL STRAND   Tailor's Apprentice, Luzzara, Italy, 1953.   28.2 x 22.3 cm.   Courtesy of The Estate of Paul Strand.   115

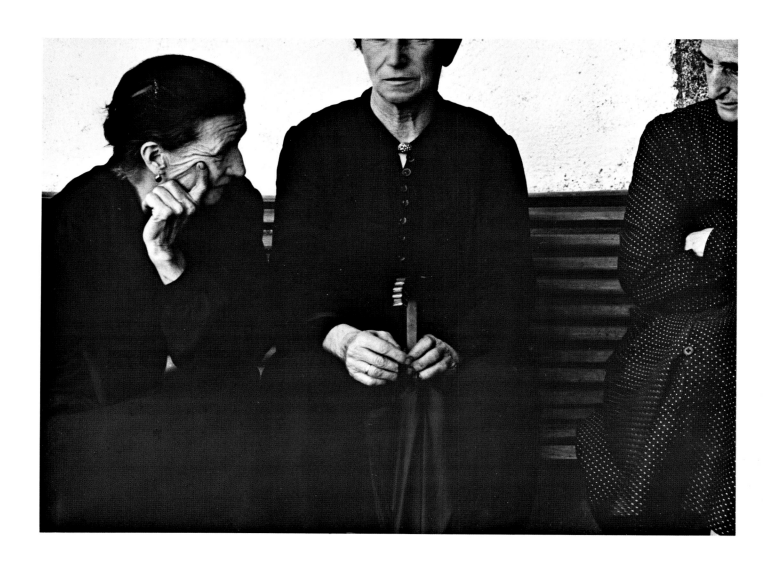

116 PAUL STRAND Women, Stes.-Maries-de-la-Mer, France, 1950. 17.8 x 24.4 cm. Courtesy of The Paul Strand Foundation.

PAUL STRAND   Hat Factory, Luzzara, Italy, 1953.   24.5 x 19.4 cm.   Courtesy of The Paul Strand Foundation.   117

118 PAUL STRAND Tir A'Mhurain, South Uist, Hebrides, 1954. 26.1 x 33.1 cm. Courtesy of The Paul Strand Foundation.

PAUL STRAND   Cattle Sale, Loch Ollay, South Uist, Hebrides, 1954.   11.7 x 14.8 cm.   Courtesy of The Estate of Paul   119
Strand.

FREDERICK SOMMER

FREDERICK SOMMER   *Circumnavigation of the Blood*, 1950.   10.3 x 14.3 cm.   Courtesy of the photographer.   121

122   FREDERICK SOMMER   Taylor, Arizona, 1945.   19.4 x 24.4 cm.   Courtesy of The Center for Creative Photography, Tucson.

WILLIAM KLEIN

124 WILLIAM KLEIN Gun 1, New York City, 1954. 32.2 x 23.2 cm. Courtesy of the photographer.

WILLIAM KLEIN   Elsa Maxwell's Toy Ball, Waldorf Astoria, New York, 1955.   26.0 x 37.9 cm.   Courtesy of the   125
photographer.

126   WILLIAM KLEIN   Dance in Brooklyn, New York, 1955.   27.4 x 37.7 cm.   Courtesy of the photographer.

WILLIAM KLEIN   Grace, New York, 1954.   25.5 x 32.9 cm.   Courtesy of the photographer.   127

WILLIAM A. GARNETT

WILLIAM A. GARNETT   Nude Dune, Death Valley, California, 1954.   34.1 x 26.4 cm.   Courtesy of the photographer.   129

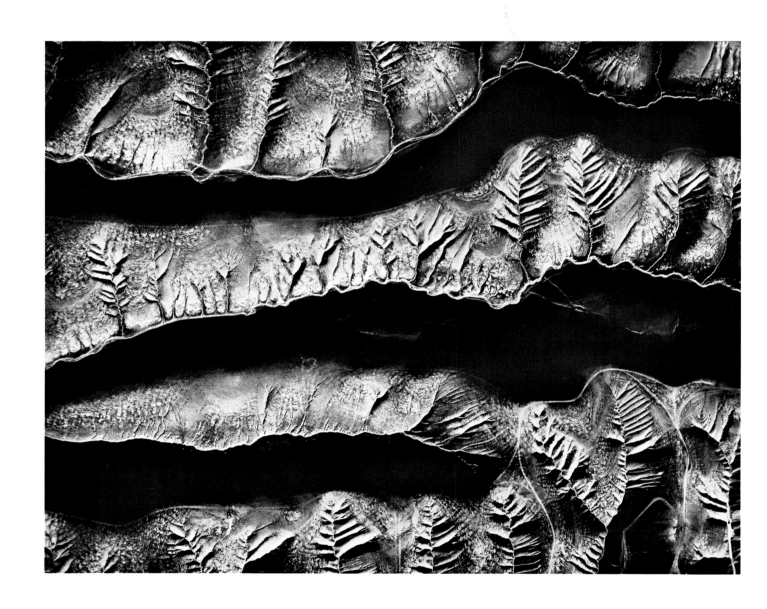

130 WILLIAM A. GARNETT Erosion, Tehachapi Foothills, California, 1951. 27.6 x 35.2 cm. Courtesy of the photographer.

HENRY HOLMES SMITH

132   HENRY HOLMES SMITH   Angels, 1952.   17.4 x 21.7 cm.   Courtesy of The Henry Holmes Smith Archive, Indiana University
Art Museum.

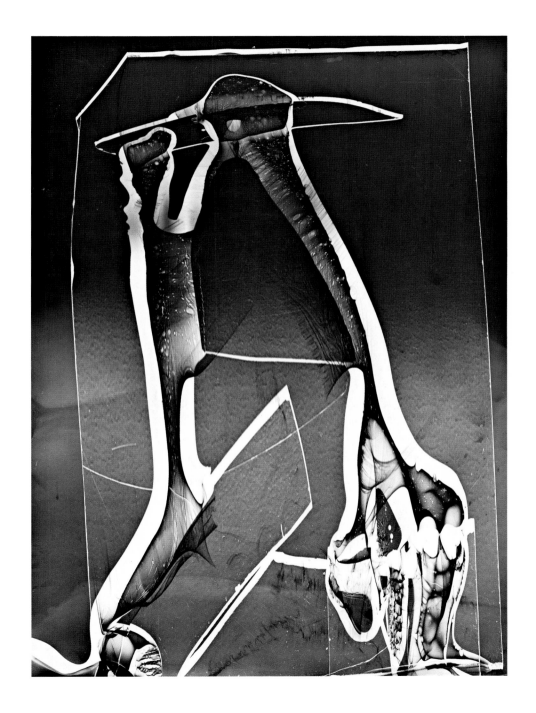

HENRY HOLMES SMITH   Growing Up I, 1952.   34.8 x 25.2 cm.   Courtesy of The Henry Holmes Smith Archive, Indiana   133
University Art Museum.

ELIOT PORTER

ELIOT PORTER   Pojoaque Valley, New Mexico, July, 1950.   17.2 x 23.5 cm.   Courtesy of the photographer.   135

136   ELIOT PORTER   Del Carmen Mountains, Big Bend, Texas, May, 1950.   17.6 x 23.7 cm.   Courtesy of the photographer.

IMOGEN CUNNINGHAM

138   IMOGEN CUNNINGHAM   Tea at Foster's, 1950.   19.4 x 17.7 cm.   Courtesy of The Center for Creative Photography, Tucson.

IMOGEN CUNNINGHAM   Self-portrait on Geary Street, 1958.   22.6 x 18.3 cm.   Courtesy of The Imogen Cunningham   139
Trust, Berkeley, California.

140 IMOGEN CUNNINGHAM Pregnant Woman, 1959. 18.9 x 19.0 cm. Courtesy of The Center for Creative
Photography, Tucson.

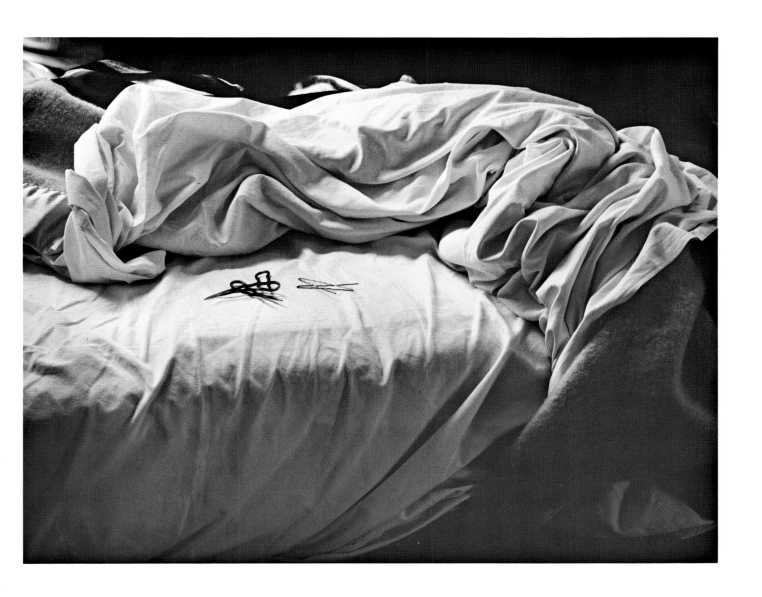

IMOGEN CUNNINGHAM   The Unmade Bed, 1957.   26.5 x 34.1 cm.   Courtesy of The Center for Creative Photography,   141
Tucson.

DAN WEINER

DAN WEINER   Bus Boycott, Montgomery, Alabama, 1956.   22.7 x 33.8 cm.   Courtesy of Sandra Weiner.   143

144   DAN WEINER   Bus Boycott, Montgomery, Alabama, 1956.   24.3 x 35.2 cm.   Courtesy of Sandra Weiner.

DAN WEINER   Martin Luther King, Bus Boycott, Montgomery, Alabama, 1956.   35.6 x 24.3 cm.   Courtesy of Sandra   145
Weiner.

ANSEL ADAMS

ANSEL ADAMS   Ice on Ellery Lake, Sierra Nevada, California, ca. 1959.   33.3 x 47.7 cm.   Courtesy of Harry H. Lunn, Jr.   147

148 ANSEL ADAMS   White Branches, Mono Lake, California, 1950.   48.4 x 37.9 cm.   Courtesy of The Lunn Gallery, Washington, D.C.

ANSEL ADAMS Aspens, Northern New Mexico, 1958. 38.8 x 49.3 cm. Courtesy of The Lunn Gallery, Washington, D.C. 149

IRVING PENN

IRVING PENN   Plumber, New York, 1951.   49.7 x 37.8 cm.   Courtesy of the photographer.   151

152   IRVING PENN   Woman with Roses, 1950.   55.2 x 37.0 cm.   Courtesy of the photographer.

IRVING PENN   Black and White *Vogue* Cover, 1950.   41.1 x 34.6 cm.   Courtesy of the photographer.   153

154   IRVING PENN   Harlequin Dress, 1950.   51.8 x 47.9 cm.   Courtesy of the photographer.

ROBERT FRANK

156   ROBERT FRANK   Political Rally, Chicago, 1956.   29.1 x 18.7 cm.   Courtesy of Mr. and Mrs. Murray H. Bring.

ROBERT FRANK Canal Street, New Orleans, 1955. 18.3 x 27.8 cm. Courtesy of The Lunn Gallery, Washington, D.C. 157

158 ROBERT FRANK Candy Store, New York City, 1955. 20.1 x 30.3 cm. Courtesy of The Lunn Gallery, Washington, D.C.

ROBERT FRANK   *Drive-in Movie, Detroit, 1955.*   20.9 x 31.7 cm.   Courtesy of The Lunn Gallery, Washington, D.C.   159

160　ROBERT FRANK　Fishkill, New York, 1955.　25.6 x 35.4 cm.　Courtesy of The Lunn Gallery, Washington, D.C.

ROBERT FRANK   Times Square, 1959.   21.4 x 32.4 cm.   Courtesy of The Lunn Gallery, Washington, D.C.   161

Index to Photographers